CORN EXCH ANGE

A GIRL IS A HALF-FORMED THING

Eimear McBride

adapted for the stage by
Annie Ryan

The Corn Exchange's production
of *A Girl Is a Half-formed Thing*
premiered as part of the
Dublin Theatre Festival
at the Samuel Beckett Centre
on 25 September 2014.

A Girl Is a Half-formed Thing

Creative team

Performer **Aoife Duffin**
Director **Annie Ryan**
Music and Sound Designer **Mel Mercier**
Set Designer **Lian Bell**
Lighting Designer **Sinéad Wallace**
Costume Designer **Katie Crowley**
Assistant Director **Eoghan Carrick**
Producer **Lucy Ryan**

International Tour Producer **Pádraig Cusack**

Production Manager **Lisa Mahony**
Stage Manager **Danny Erskine**
Chief LX **Kevin Smith**
Sound Engineer **Alexis Nealon**
Production Assistant **Rachel Bergin**

Touring team

Production Manager **Adrain Mullen**
Chief LX **Kevin Smith**
Sound Engineer **Anthony Hanley**

Graphic Design Photography **Richie Gilligan**
Production Photography **Fiona Morgan**
Graphic Design **Aad**

Biographies

Eimear McBride Writer

Eimear McBride grew up in Sligo and Mayo. At seventeen, she moved to London to study acting at Drama Centre. At twenty-seven she wrote *A Girl Is a Half-formed Thing* and spent most of the next decade trying to have it published. Eventually picked up by Galley Beggar Press in Norwich, it went on to win the Baileys Women's Prize for Fiction, the Desmond Elliot Prize, Kerry Group Irish Novel of the Year and the inaugural Goldsmiths Prize. She is working on her second novel.

Annie Ryan Adaptor and Director

Annie Ryan was born and raised in Chicago, trained there as an actor at the Piven Theatre Workshop and became a member of Chicago's renegade *commedia dell'arte* company, New Crime. She received a BFA in Acting from NYU's Tisch School of the Arts. These combined vocabularies formed the foundation of her work with The Corn Exchange, founded in 1995. Annie has directed all of the company's productions to date, including modern classics, adaptations and original works created in collaboration with writer Michael West.

Aoife Duffin

Aoife trained at the Samuel Beckett centre at Trinity College, Dublin. Theatre work has included *Spring Awakening* (Headlong); *The Crucible* (Lyric Theatre, Belfast); *Christ Deliver Us!* (Abbey Theatre, Dublin); *The Silver Tassie* (Druid); *The Importance of Being Earnest* and *Solemn Mass for a Full Moon in the Summer* (Rough Magic); *The Crumb Trail* and *Oedipus Loves You* (Pan Pan Theatre); and *Little Gem* (Guna Nua). Televison work has included: *Moone Boy* (Sky). Film work has included *Earthbound* (Ripplewood Pictures); *Out of Here* (Stalker Films); *What Richard Did* (Element Pictures); *Behold the Lamb* (Film Four); *Joy* (Venom Films); *Fear of Flying* (Animation); and *When Harvey Met Bob* (BBC).

Mel Mercier Composer and Sound Designer

Composer, performer, academic and teacher, Mel is Head of the
School of Music and Theatre, University College Cork (UCC). He has
performed and collaborated with pianist and composer Mícheál Ó
Súilleabháin for over thirty years and is director of the Cork Gamelan
Ensemble.

Composition and sound design for theatre includes: *The Testament of
Mary* (Barbican and Broadway – NY Drama Desk Award and Tony
Award nomination); *Desire Under the Elms* (Corn Exchange); Fiona
Shaw/Phyllida Lloyd's *The Rime of the Ancient Mariner* (Old Vic, BAM,
Bouffes du Nord); and performances of John Cage's *Roaratorio: An
Irish Circus on Finnegans Wake* (Cage Centenary); *Sétanta* (Abbey);
School for Scandal (Barbican); *The East Pier / The Passing* (Abbey);
Man of Aran (Once Off Productions); *Mother Courage* (National
Theatre, London); *Happy Days* (National Theatre); *The Hour We Knew
Nothing of Each Another* (National Theatre); *Julius Caesar* (Barbican);
Fewer Emergencies (Royal Court); *Medea* (Abbey).

Lian Bell Set Designer

Since completing an MA in Scenography at Central St Martin's,
London, in 2002, Lian has worked in Dublin as a set designer, arts
manager, and artistic collaborator with some of the most significant
arts organisations and contemporary performance makers. She has
designed for performances by Moonfish Theatre (*Star of the Sea*),
Brokentalkers (*In Real Time, Silver Stars, This Is Still Life*), Catapult
Dance (*Did I Make You Up?, Walk Don't Run, You are Here, Beatbox
Bingo*) and Junk Ensemble (*Drinking Dust*). Lian is collaborating with
director Una McKevitt on research ideas for two new productions,
including a reimagining of O'Neill's *A Long Day's Journey into Night*
and work in progress with circus artist Emily Aoibheann on a presentation
titled *Dying Breeds*.

Katie Crowley Costume Designer

Katie studied Costume Design for Stage and Screen at IADT. Since
graduating she has worked as costume designer on *Love Song and
Dance* by Cois Ceim; *Broadreach, Marvel* by Eala Productions and
Best Man by the Everyman. She has worked as wardrobe supervisor

for *Borstal Boy* and *Moll* at the Gaiety Theatre, *Agnes* by Cois Ceim, *A Particle of Dread* by Field Day Productions and *Desire Under the Elms* by the Corn Exchange. Katie has also worked as a costume assistant for the Gate Theatre on *An Ideal Husband*, *The Vortex*, *A Streetcar Named Desire*, *Mrs Warren's Profession* and *A Woman of No Importance*.

Sinéad Wallace Lighting Designer

Sinéad graduated in 2004 from Trinity College, where she studied Drama and Theatre. She received Irish Times Theatre Awards for Best Lighting in 2010 for *Happy Days* (Corn Exchange), in 2009 for *Knives in Hens* (Landmark) and in 2007 for *Saved* (Abbey Theatre) and *Don Carlos* (Rough Magic). This is Sinéad's third outing with Corn Exchange, having previously lit *Desire Under the Elms* (DTF 2013) and *Happy Days*. Sinéad's other previous lighting designs include *A Tender Thing* (Siren Productions), *Body and Forgetting* (Liz Roche Dance Co.), *Christ Deliver Us*, *La Dispute*, *The Seafarer*, *and True West* (Abbey Theatre), *Miss Julie* (Landmark Productions), *Ellamenope Jones*, *Fewer Emergencies*, *The Public*, *The Drowned World and The Illusion* (Randolf SD | The Company) and *The Mental* (Little John Nee).

Lucy Ryan Producer

Lucy has a background in the theatre, film and TV industries in both Ireland and the UK. After working at the Donmar Warehouse Theatre, London, for a number of years, she moved into script development for the UK film and television industry, working for a number of large production houses including Pathe Pictures, the UK Film Council and the Irish Film Board as well as lecturing on script editing at Goldsmiths University of London. In 2011 she refocused on theatre with the help of the Step Change programme run by the National Theatre and worked as producer with a variety of organisations including Artichoke on the 2011 Lumière event in Durham and with LIFT on a large-scale outdoor spectacular as part of the London 2012 festival. In late 2012 Lucy returned to Dublin and started working with The Corn Exchange, producing both *Desire Under the Elms* for the 2013 Dublin Theatre Festival and *A Girl Is a Half-formed Thing*. She is currently working with Corn Exchange on the 2015–2016 programme.

CORN EXCH ANGE

Founded by Annie Ryan in 1995, The Corn Exchange has created an award-winning repertoire, ranging from contemporary site-specific work, adaptations of classics and original theatre made in collaboration with the ensemble and writer Michael West.

The company combines a strong physical theatre practice with dynamic text to create highly imaginative, transformational theatre. The company has toured work all over Ireland and the UK, France, Germany, Poland, Australia, The US and Mexico.

Recent work includes:
Desire Under the Elms by Eugene O'Neill
Dubliners by James Joyce, adapted by Michael West and Annie Ryan, co-produced with Dublin Theatre Festival
Man of Valour by Michael West, Annie Ryan and Paul Reid.
Happy Days by Samuel Beckett
Cat on a Hot Tin Roof by Tennessee Williams
Freefall, Everyday and Dublin by Lamplight by Michael West in collaboration with the company.

Among numerous awards over the years including a Best Actress nominaton for Aoife Duffin in *A Girl Is a Half-formed Thing* , awards for the company include Irish Times Theatre Awards for Best Lighting Design for Sinead Wallace for *Happy Days*, Best Director and Best Writer for *Freefall* and Best Production for *Mud* by Irene Fornes.

For more information on our workshops and productions visit cornexchange.ie or follow us on Twitter @Thecornexchange or Facebook.

Artistic Director: **Annie Ryan**
Executive Producer: **Lucy Ryan**
Associate Director: **Eoghan Carrick**

Board of Directors
Ross Keane (Chair)
Trevor Bowen   **Deobrah Dignam**
Pádraig Heneghan   **Louise O'Reilly**
Teresa McGrane   **Kathy Scott**

The Corn Exchange would like to thank:

The Arts Council, Dublin City Council, Culture Ireland, Ulster Bank, Bobbie Bergin, Carol McMahon, Sinead McHugh, Cian O'Brien and all at The Project Arts Centre, Gillian Mitchell and all at the MAC, Niamh O'Brien and all at Mermaid Arts Centre, Willie White and all at the Dublin Theatre Festival, Leinster Cricket Club, Danny Erskine, Clare Howe, Rachel Bergin, Louise Doyle, Tracey Elliston, Catriona Ennis, Erica Murray, Michael West, Thomas and Oliver West, John and Cecily West, Michael Hinds and Christine West, Kerry West and Jason King, Jonathan Wheeler, Jack Phelan, Pat and Joan Ryan, Lisa McLaughlin, Kay Scorah and David Keating, Rory Gilmartin, William Galinsky and The Corn Exchange Board of Directors.

The Corn Exchange is supported by The Arts Council of Ireland and Dublin City Council. International touring has been supported by Culture Ireland.

Comhairle Cathrach
Bhaile Átha Cliath
Dublin City Council

Culture Ireland
Cultúr Éireann

The Corn Exchange operates in partnership with Ulster Bank.

⠭Ulster Bank

A Girl Is a Half-formed Thing

Eimear McBride grew up in Sligo and Mayo. At seventeen she moved to London to study acting at Drama Centre. At twenty-seven she wrote *A Girl Is a Half-formed Thing* and spent most of the next decade trying to have it published. It was eventually picked up by Galley Beggar Press in Norwich, and went on to win the Baileys Women's Prize for Fiction, the Desmond Elliot Prize, Kerry Group Irish Novel of the Year and the inaugural Goldsmiths Prize. She is working on her second novel.

Annie Ryan was born and raised in Chicago, trained there as an actor at the Piven Theatre Workshop and became a member of Chicago's renegade *commedia dell'arte* company, New Crime. She received a BFA in Acting from NYU's Tisch School of the Arts. These combined vocabularies formed the foundation of her work with The Corn Exchange, founded in 1995. Annie has directed all the company's productions to date, including modern classics, adaptations and original works created in collaboration with writer Michael West.

EIMEAR MCBRIDE

A Girl Is a Half-Formed Thing

Adapted for the stage by
Annie Ryan

FABER & FABER

First published in 2015
by Faber and Faber Limited
74–77 Great Russell Street
London WC1B 3DA

First published in the US in 2016

Typeset by Country Setting, Kingsdown, Kent CT14 8ES
Printed in England by CPI Group (UK) Ltd, Croydon CR0 4YY

A CIP record for this book
is available from the British Library

ISBN 978-0-571-32579-5

FSC
www.fsc.org
MIX
Paper from
responsible sources
FSC® C013604

4 6 8 10 9 7 5 3

A Girl Is a Half-formed Thing by Eimear McBride was adapted for the stage by Annie Ryan and first produced by the Corn Exchange Theatre Company at the Samuel Beckett Centre, Trinity College Dublin, as part of Dublin Theatre Festival, on 25 September 2014.

Girl Aoife Duffin

Adaptor and Director Annie Ryan
Music and Sound Designer Mel Mercier
Set Designer Lian Bell
Lighting Designer Sinéad Wallace
Costume Designer Katie Crowley
Assistant Director Eoghan Carrick
Producer Lucy Ryan

Foreword

Eimear McBride's book *A Girl Is a Half-formed Thing* landed on my kitchen table like a gift from the gods. Actually, it was from my husband, who is friendly with Eimear McBride's husband, William Galinsky. They visited our house together one dark winter's night some years ago when William was director of the Cork Midsummer Festival. One buys one's friend's wife's book. And there it was. I had been searching for a project to do with my company, so, to avoid reading yet another play, I took it to bed. At about four in the morning I was sitting bolt up, gasping in horror as the novel came to its breathtaking close. I was electrified, exhilarated. But here's what I said out loud – loud enough to wake up my husband: 'It's performable.'

I knew this partly because to make sense of it in the first few chapters, I had to read it out loud – not loud enough to wake anyone, just quietly, to myself. We found out from audience members later on that this is a common enough act among readers. People read it out loud. It wants to be heard.

I first got in touch with Eimear with a simple proposal: to present the story as a one-woman show in some kind of abstract Beckettian landscape.

I might have felt it was performable, but whether it was stagable was another question. I knew the embodiment of the characters would have to be handled very carefully, to somehow prioritise the voice rather than the picture. Eimear agreed. In fact in one meeting, she told me, after being presented with various photographs of slighted ravaged young women by an American magazine article, she said, 'We're inside of her head, so it is very important that we never see her.' 'Yes. Yes,' I nodded, 'But we are going to have to cast her!'

Aoife Duffin immediately came to mind. Aoife's a very experienced leading stage actress with incredible range and sensitivity, a deep alto register and a fabulous Kerry accent. Her ability to fully embody the work with such power and subtlety was astonishing and humbling. I am very grateful to her for her bravery and her extremely hard work. It was an upsetting text to speak, especially in the early days of rehearsal, and without doubt a harrowing piece to learn and live with. I can't imagine anyone else performing it, but I suppose now, with this book, people will.

There is a lot of trauma in this story. I feel the trauma is somewhat countered by the incredible aliveness of the language and the acute awareness of the Girl herself. She absolutely owns her experience with genuine courage and an unapologetic sense of her own agency. Even when she is causing herself harm or terrible things are happening to her, she perseveres to find her own truth, without rancour, without self-pity. And while this piece points to a legacy of cruelty and oppression, it springs from the deep love she has for her brother and her rage about his illness, his difference, his loss. The text is written with such an exquisitely felt sense of what is happening from moment to moment that anyone undertaking this project needs to hold the material, the actor and the audience with great care.

Finally I think one of the most radical things about this piece is simply the fact of it being about and from the mind of a girl. It's a shockingly sad fact that it is so rare to hear a female voice, both in literature and on our stages and screens. Indian film director Mira Nair created a film training centre in Uganda with this motto: 'If we don't tell our stories, no one else will.'

I'd like to take this opportunity to thank in print the many people who helped this piece come to fruition. Theatre is, of course, a deeply collaborative art, and I am so grateful for the care and contribution these people gave me and the project. Thanks to my husband, Michael West, for the book. And while we were frantically searching for the costume, for giving us his pyjamas. I thank him mostly for his love and for teaching me so much about writing for the theatre.

And I'd like to thank my company: my producer, Lucy Ryan, whose expertise as a former script editor was extremely appreciated; Eoghan Carrick, my brilliant assistant director; Danny Erskine and later Clare Howe, who took great care of Aoife and the team through the process; our excellent design team, composer Mel Mercier, set designer Lian Bell, lighting designer Sinéad Wallace and costume designer Katie Crowley; the brilliant Lisa Mahony, our production assistant Rachel Bergin, our technical team Adrian Mullen, Kevin Smith, Alexis Nealon, Anthony Hanley, photographers Richie Gilligan and Fiona Morgan and our graphic designers Scott Burnett and Brian Heffernan at Aad. Thanks to Willie White and Dublin Theatre Festival for presenting us over the last few years and to Pádraig Cusack for his endorsement and help in bringing our work to the world.

Thank you to The Corn Exchange Board of Directors for their support and encouragement to make the bravest artistic choices; Bobby Bergin and Carol McMahon at Ulster Bank for supporting the company and this production; to Culture Ireland, Dublin City Council and particularly the Arts Council of Ireland, without whose funding I wouldn't be a theatre maker.

Thanks to all my teachers, my family, Michael's family and our sons for their patience for my lack of attention and their encouragement of me in my work. May you grow up to be good feminists.

I'm especially grateful to Eimear McBride who allowed me to slice up her stunning book with such severity. Although she did admit that she prefers the eight-hour unabridged version (you can hear Eimear read the audio book), she gave her us blessing with total grace and generosity, recognising that we were transforming her incredible work into something else, and giving it another life.

In the theatre, long life is rare. Great effort is made to give a show a decent run, but eventually, and usually all too soon, it dies. It's terribly exciting that this work can exist on a shelf in this form – as a book. Obviously, it cannot touch the original in terms of intimacy, detail, breadth, but this version isn't meant for the solo reader. It's designed to be experienced in a room full of other people. In one go. And in that context, it only really comes alive again in front of an audience. It is for them. For them to bear witness.

Annie Ryan
Dublin, March 2015

Note on the Adaptation

This adaptation was conceived for a solo performer on a spare set with no props or furniture.

Whereas the dialogue in the original text is rarely attributed to character and only indicated through spacing in one scene in the entire book, I have used line breaks to point to dialogue as well as shifts in character, time and location. The novel's chapter headings are also included here to help the performer and creative team to understand the arc of the narrative, but there is no sign of these breaks in performance. The piece runs straight through for approximately eighty minutes.

AR

A GIRL IS A HALF-FORMED THING

PART I
Lambs

For you. You'll soon. You'll give her name. In the stitches of her skin she'll wear your say.

Mammy me?

Yes you.

Bounce the bed, I'd say. I'd say that's what you did. Then lay you down. They cut you round. Wait and hour and day.

Are you alright? Will you sit, he says.

No. I want she says. I want to see my son.

Her heart going pat. Going dum dum dum. Smell from Dettol through her skin.

Jesus. Oh no.

We done the best we could. It's all through his brain like the roots of trees.

Can't you operate again?

We can't.

Something?

Chemo then. We'll have a go at that.

Gethsemane dear Lord hear our prayer our. Please don't God take. Our.

Feel fat juicy poison poison young boy skin. Weeks for you. Weeks it. Scared and bald and wet the bed.

There's good news and bad news. It's shrunk.

He's saved.

But we'll never be rid do you understand?

Shush now she says shush.

I'd give my eyes to fix him but. The heart cannot be wrung and wrung.

What're you saying? Going? Leaving? But he's just stopped dying. This one's to come. Please don't no I won't stop you. You'll support us. Aren't you great? Oh the house is mine. Oh so kind. Aren't you the fine shape of a man.

Where's Daddy?

Gone.

Why's that?

Just is.

Look.

Poke belly of baby that's kicking is me. I loved swimming to your touch. Your strokes. Secret pressed hellos. Show my red foot.

Baby when you're born I pick your name.

Scream to rupture day.

There now a girleen isn't she great.

But I saw less with these flesh eyes. Outside almost without sight.

I'm so glad your brother's lived. That he'll see you. It'll all be.

But. Something's coming. Wiping off my begans. Wiping all my every time. I struggle up to. I struggle from. The smell of milk now. Going dim. Going blank. Going white.

2

Two me. Four you five or so. Baby full of snot and tears. You squeeze on my sides just a bit. I retch up awful tickle giggs.

I flee from washing brushing. I am

Boldness incarnate, little madam little miss. Don't you want hair like your brother's? Out in handfuls but two years on – as good as you.

3

Now when you are seven eight. Me five.

You and me having slug scum races from the doorway to the source where is it.

Get a jam jar get it.

Stuck in that twig.

Never you ever touch it. Never. Ever. Touch. That. Dirty. Thing. It'll. Give. You. Warts. That. Is. Di. Sgust. Ing.

Godforsaken house it is look out it's lashing down. Whose is that car? Oh God let it not be the PP and the state of the place. Don't pull the curtain back. Go wipe your nose you.

Daddy. I didn't recognise you. You gave me the fright of my life. Surely you didn't do all that drive today?

Come in here and say hello to your grandfather. He's come all the way to see you, isn't that right? You know, I haven't a thing in the house. Sure I wasn't expecting you. I'll just nip out. You tell Granda the result of your IQ test. Average. Now isn't that good? It is. No of course I'm glad you came. Look let me go get these few things in.

Sit down youngster and tell me what have you been at since I was here last. What class are you in? Have you been saying your prayers? Going to communion? And confession? Every week? So why do you not go more often or are you just so good? You know pride's a deadly sin. Your father was a proud man. He wouldn't come to mass and look what happened to you as a result. Well now, say a Hail Mary and we'll forget about it but the next time you go you tell the priest. Go on then. Hail Mary. Go on Hail Mary full of . . . Grace. You pick it up. The Lord is . . . How can you forget? Do you not say the rosary in this house? Then how can you not know the Hail Mary?

And what about you Miss Piggy? That snout you have on you. Don't you hit your grandfather. Bold brat. Now I'll have to tell your mother and you'll get a beat on your bot. Because I'm her daddy so if I say it she has to give you a smack.

I've just been talking to your son. And that child only made his communion a year ago and he can't even say his Hail Mary.

And look at that one. Forward rolls in a skirt. It's disgusting. Underwear on display. How is she supposed to be a child of Mary?

There must be something wrong with you. You're not right in the head. Well it's little wonder why your husband left. If I had to live with this kind of godlessness going on under my roof. No. I cannot stay. God forgive me I never knew I'd reared a . . . No. Enough. That's it. Goodbye.

Are you pleased with yourselves? What did I say about forward rolls? What did I tell you about keeping your knickers covered?

She is jumping up the stairs. Take one and two. Crack my eyes are bursting from my head with the wallop. Blood rising up my nose.

You. Panic.

Mammy sorry that I sorry I didn't know.

Hail Mary. How hard can it be? Hail Mary. School for morons is where you belong and you can live there and you can do what you like and I'll never have to put up with you again. Selfish spoilt brats.

Mammy my head. Mammy my my don't Mammy hit me any more on my my

Tomato soup we made.

Put it down there.

Mammy here's your dinner. We'll be good from now on and do everything you say. Please don't send me to handicap school.

4

Me and the stink girls when we are playing. Our altar decked with cottonbud candelabra. Jesus wafer cheese and onion.

Through him with him in him in the unity of the Holy Spirit. This is the body of Christ and eat your crisp.

And on her mother push the door we quick disband for blasphemy's the fatal sin.

Give that to your mam a ghrá. We're the Charismatics. Doing the good work. Doing the good work for Christ Our Lord.

And she came one Sunday evening and she said every Thursday then. Six o'clock?

Yes. Fine.

They come with fruitcakes. Brown-skin nylons.
Leatherette shoes. They pray to God and pray and pray
for God's sake to be saved. They're swaying rolling.
Palms out rigid. Letting in the Holy Spirit.

Mammy I have to go toilet.

Inside under Jesus I make my dash out in the rain. Slap
mud all up my socks. I'll skid it. Scutter it. Being magic.
Saying fucker Christ. Into the fields. My bad words best
collection. Stupid shit fuck piss cow bitch frigger shiter
fucker bitch pig. All the things my mother never taught
me. To shit in a field or run in from the rain. So I knew it
always then and do it all the time. Oh crouch. Dock leaf.
Plopped. True I could be killed for that. And a white one
too. Should not have been licking chalk.

PART II
A Girl Is a Half-formed Thing

The beginning of teens us. Thirteen me fifteen sixteen you. Wave and wave of it hormone over.

Imagination of fathers sitting by me on the bed. Stroking my hair you're my girl, belong to me pet. And I say will you ever tell me what he said about daughters before I was born?

I've something to tell you after all. Your father's hmmm. Your father's, sit down.

What?

Dead. A while ago I got a letter from his mother. She said he took a stroke.

But you never told us? Why didn't you tell us?

There wasn't much I could say, not like he loved you, us I mean. You're provided for. It's time to go about our business.

What's that?

Moving house.

Why?

Because he bought this and I don't want it any more.

But I don't want to move Mammy.

We're. Moving. House. Because. That. Is. What. I'd. Like. To. Do. And. If. You. Don't. Too. Bad. Because. I'm. The. Mother. And. You. Will. Do. What. I. Say. As.

Long. As. You. Live. Under. My. Roof. You. Will. Always. Do. What. I. Say. O. Kay.

Do you like the look of that school? There. That's where you'll be going. Now. Both. For the first time. Isn't that nice?

We sliced through that fug school bus.

I be new girl. I could wish to be dead but for the wrong of it.

Those herd. Such bovine singing heifers.

New girl stinks.

I see you.

Come down here new boy.

Gunk you.

Ha ha ha spastic. Spastic fall over. Can't spastic walk?

I feel it gone, my fucker Jesus self. It weep away like longed for wound. No nothing there. No badness to keep me. Prop me up.

What happened you there?

Where?

That big scar on your head.

You say, and shock me, a knife did it.

Is that true? Did it hurt?

A little bit you say.

Were you really cut?

Yes awful deep is why my eye's not so good.

And was there much blood?

Oh loads.

And did they think you'd die?

They did. Somehow I didn't.

Did they go to court?

They got away.

They got away. With it?

From the country, thickorwhat, you say.

Oh right. Oh right yeah.

I smelt it go around the school all day.

Hey dimwit shitfit what happened your brother? What
happened his head?

Sweat me down my polyester pinafore. Don't want to get
into it. I don't want to burst your lie.

Bus home you were not tripped up. And no one said
thicko fuck-up shitehawk. And you sat with the cool lads
on the bus.

2

Say hello to your aunt and uncle.

Our mother's sister she. To call. To come and stay.

Ah he'll not be tall like his Da oh should I not? His father
was a tall man after all.

I look at him. I look him back from looking right at me.
Uncle uncle. I'll stare you dare you and don't think
you're posh than better than us.

We have a lovely awkward dinner of gammon and
mashed spud.

My girls won't touch it. Pork is such a, you know meat.

Did you get the cheque? Did you get that cheque she kept saying to her I keep forgetting if I've asked? Yabber yabber.

Hmm and yes and is that right?

My two are off to the convent. As long as they have their degrees. Shop-floor management or whatever history. Degrees the thing and tra la la – what are the chances yours'll do that?

I'm spitting.

Oh are they really aunt and uncle how was it they got in the convent when they only got D's. Just lucky? Didn't you pay for them in? You cow come here eat your tea and say we're all these sorts of things.

Go to your room. Go right there now. I mean it.

I'm flooding the hallway up those stairs.

Fuck off. You snobs. Bastards.

Till the back door click. They have gone out. And you went with them I know.

Tap on my door. Tap tapping he uncle push it through.

Are you alright? Thought I'd see if you're.

I'm fine.

That's quite a moment to treat us to and on the first day.

I know it.

Can I come in?

Alright, do.

Your aunt's a bit of a . . . She's very fond of you, underneath.

Nice way to show it.

I'll have a word about. Sorry.

I know she's your wife but I don't like her.

You're a funny girl.

Why's that then?

Cheeky madam.

Maybe I am.

Oh you are.

Well that's me.

Good for you can I ask you.

What?

Do you climb out that window to meet your boyfriends at night?

We went to school. In the cold lunch break they are kicking football on the muck pitch. Your little limp.

Hey lads what's going on?

How did you get your scar again?

A knife.

A knife? Oh was it? I heard you got your brain cut up.

Did not.

That you're brain-damaged.

I am not.

You're a brain-damaged liar.

No listen you said. Listen lads.

Uuuuuggggh. Handicap. Handicap.

I close my eyes and wish this day had never been or you or me. Pretend I didn't even see.

I ride the bus. You don't say a word. I will not think of you. I think. Uncle. Must move or shake him. I must give him some surprise.

And in the kitchen I see him there. You go drag foot.

Hi Aunt Mammy.

Their hellos to me. I going. Keep going. Not my single word for him.

It ran up me. Legs knees chest up head. I'd throw up excitement.

Don't be fucked-up.

Are you hiding from me? You haven't said a word in days. What did I do?

Nothing.

Did I offend you?

No. Sorry I.

I see you. I see you very clear. I do. So come here. And I can't help wondering if you see me? You see, I think you do.

I'm invaded in my ears by pulse is going round and round.

You are. Oh you're a strange one but I see you. For. What. You. Are. And do you know there's no one home?

I am sweating here. Ready to give and not.

I want to kiss you.

He put his mouth on mine. Then. Wave of. Lost.

That was nice but don't you want to kiss me back?

I.

I'd like you to open your mouth a bit.

I. Do. With lips and teeth and with his tongue.

Fill my mouth with it.

Is this the first kiss you've had at all?

Flexed and on a wire I'm. Feel I might begin to cry or sink or fall.

Don't be angry with me he says. I'm very very honoured.

I am what I should do? My hand. On his trousers. I feel. Stroke.

No! Not for me. I am not. I'm not that man.

I'm clammy sweat. And legs are wrong. Excused and dismissed. What I say is

You fuck off.

Come running by the lake. Eyes mist to the wind feel the fresh rush past. That new day it's so early in the morning.

I step there. Cool and cold and colder. Coming in over my white socks.

It soak my coat up. Up my leg up. Feel it there inside my thigh.

I sink baptise me now O Lord and take this bloody itch away for what am I the wrong and wrong of it always always far from thee. In this world deep and brown. You are not here. I am free from love and that cold pain shooting through my forehead.

I'm floating downside up and wrong side down.

Slipping grapple blackthorn bush to pull me out. I see my sorry self. I don't think I will be clean now. Think instead I'll have revenge for lots of all kinds of things.

The house is dry and creaky. I am sopping on the floor. I hear him. I know that step.

What have you done? You're wet the whole way through. What did you?

Fell in the lake.

How strange my baptise renders me. His want me. Fuck me if he could and I and I and I. I have that. And I do not. Do not need. Have something else I need to do. I left him dripping in the door. Ha. He did not get me after all.

Oh but he did. I'm lying. I am not I am. By the cold range in my white drip shirt. Caught me. Went about me tooth and claw that I wanted. Pull my skirt down by ankles. Shed. And it was so quiet all around that I could hear him open me. Graze me opening my legs.

I'm splashing falling into it.

And this is what it's like after all. After all I've heard. It hurts me. Too much so much. It. Is too much then. My back against the chair wood. Rubbing to the bone. I. He is coming. Off inside me. I must be almost I am dying when he does it. With the pain.

He says. Alright?

I am dripping water, him, out on my thigh.

Are you alright?

I am. I am pure white.

He says You're going to be fine. It's just a shock when. The first time. Just be calm. Just be calm. Pat me on the back. You're fine. You'll be fine. Why don't you go and have a wash he says. I'll put the kettle on. Make some tea would you like that?

Quiet bathroom. My fingerful of goop what is it I know sperm. Like snot or phlegm. Sniffs strange. That's good and exciting. And pubic hair that's longer blacker thick than mine. I'll wash me. And my hair and everything to be clean. But butcher's block. I felt between my legs would look like that. It's an awful lot of sore.

When I went down there were cornflakes toast and jam for me and tea and anything I would want.

I've never done that before. God what's that hey that what we done?

I look at him think you've fucked me. What if they all knew what. We. He and me. That's something very new.

Then later in the day. They just went.

We are days. Watching telly drifting by.

We were moving off now. From each other. You and me were never this. This boy and girl that do not speak. But somehow I've left you behind and you're just looking on.

3

Fifteen sixteen. Eat coleslaw sandwiches with ham on top.

Me and my friend on the mitch.

We take off early she and me to down the lake and we sit in the grasses down beside the water's edge.

Sounds of boots. Hoarse laughing and shoving push.

Prick up. It's the lads.

Hey what's that book you're reading there? God how can you read books at all? Three hundred pages. Ye two are always really strange.

Sure you don't know either of us I say.

When did we last speak to any of ye.

I'm needled now wishing they would go away. I leave her for she loves to flirt it seems. Shallow stupid bitch.

What's up with you?

I'm just going for a walk.

Hey aren't you the sister of yer man in our year?

Behind me in the thicket.

The fella with the head thing. Yeah you are his sister I know you alright. You go on the bus with him or sometimes don't you?

My brother's got a little scar on his forehead if that's what you mean.

Except it's not that little, and all that bullshit story about the knife.

Fucking scum and bastards and thicko pig-ignorant culchies. Think they're all so cool and can piss on me and my brother but really they're just desperate for someone anyone to give them a wank.

Do you know how to fuck?

What?

Opened my knees said come on. You're a big hard man. You know don't you know everything.

I don't he says.

Oh don't you?

He tries. He cannot get it in. I twist myself around. He did for a little while and it feels like nothing inside me. He gulp say sorry sorry at the end.

I didn't think you'd be a virgin. Jesus. Well someone had to do it for you. Booky booky me.

Now I know full well what I can do. For me and for you.

One in the bike shed. Handlebars dig in my back. He's all embarrassed I should know the fat spots on his thighs. I'm thinking counting ticking off. The great work. It's my great work. It makes me laugh. That guzzle and the useless whinging come of them.

There is no Jesus here these days just Come all you fucking lads. I'll have you every one any day. Breakfast dinner lunch and tea.

But that one day. A Saturday. On your blue bike you come breakily up the drive. Beet-faced boiled up ready to go.

What?

Well you'd know about dirty things you say.

What's that supposed to mean?

Please tell me if it's true. You know. That you. Do all that? Dirty stuff. Dirty things. That you did the it the thing with one of the lads from my year. That you did it during lunchtime in the bogs with some other. That someone saw you down the lake.

Who told you that?

Is it true though? Is it? Is it?

Fuck off.

That's not the answer. Go on tell me if it's true? Don't you lie. You don't lie here. Is it true? Go on slut say that it's so.

What do you want?

Is it true?

It is!

You choke me.

It is disgusting whore sputter filthy disgusting wrong it's wrong to. Do. Fucking bitch.

What in God's name are you doing to your sister? Stop it. Dear God in heaven stop it. This no way to behave. You'll never make a priest like this.

I don't want to be a priest a fucking fucking fucking priest.

That's no way to talk my boy as though you're on TV.

I want to escape I want to get away from the pair of ye. I want to be in the SAS.

Packed in and up that life between my thighs.

Can I meet you round the back at lunch?

Just fuck off. You all can.

August comes. All your exams the same.

Oh what. Oh what. What will you do? Eighteen years and no exam.

Stacking shelves for you. And after one year. And after two. You are all calmed down to stacking neatly every day. Cursed and resigned.

I get my 'A's and 'B's. Go head first. On the train. With my fingers sticking out.

Bye then. Bye.

PART III
Land under the Waves

I

City all that black in my lungs. Like I'm smoking I'm not but still. I'll have a creaky bed up in some woman's house.

Going in the college door hello.

Just over there.

Fine thanks.

Yeah yeah yeah when I was in the States this summer.

Hi and how are you are you here for this course too?

What? Oh yes aha I am yes too.

This one's talking. An awful lot.

Are you living near?

Just around the corner.

I'm from here she says.

Oh right.

Coming coming?

What?

For a drink you must, course you can go on she says.

Na no thanks I don't na no well alright I will.

Stinking still she smoking Silk Cut Red. Saying her family and crazy dad's a famous writer

I haven't heard

but then but then. Groggeldy when they lived in Sweden fighting over opera seats and drinking schnapps. So boring.

And me? Nothing really. No my family's just the. You know. Like everyone else apart from you.

We are bad her. She and me. My friend I'd call.

See here this party. It's a mad. People pouring noise out front back of this old house.

Do you mind if I sit who are you then?

Some man with black hair combed strange like balding but not.

You want some? Go on lassy you inhale and hold.

In the morning peel up eyes sweat shut. Cracked ceiling somewhere.

What's the wherm I? Who? Lying. Man beside. God. Oh yes. Yuck. Sweaty eye paps fill sinus guck. And he is balding in the light. Time to go my separate ways.

Thanks yeah bye don't call.

What if. I could. I could make. A whole other world a whole civilisation in this this city that is not home? But I can. And I can choose this. And no one's falling into hell.

In the new world I am do this every single time I can.

Nicer is not what I am after. Fuck me softly fuck me quick is all the same once done to me.

That's rank. Disgusting. You dirty slut.

Dancing up upon the tables. Unbuttoning our tops.

35

Throw our knickers in the air.

Fuck you. Suck you. Ha ha ha. As though we care for we are we are Boo!

2

At Christmas.

Hello. Hello. Yes I dyed it.

Those mash potatoes I like. At home with mince meat and peas. Burned. It catch me in the throat choke good.

You're so sullen I say what's up with you?

The computer game's stuck in the tape thing.

See this fella he kicks him. See now. Hit. That button. Go on. Now. Now. Left one right one that's it now and more forward get the hang.

Not you too now. Off at that. Playing computers thought you had more sense.

Mammy don't start.

Don't you be cheeky. I know you look down on me but I'll not have irreverence from. You especially. You're not too big.

To? To what? Mammy? Is something wrong while I'm not around? What's the matter?

He's got this job and he won't drive but won't get a lift with yer one and he won't give me his pay now and won't move to his own and he won't help around the house and worst off he won't come for prayers or on Sunday go to mass says Jesus shove it up his rear I never reared ye to speak like that sometimes I wish your father hadn't died I know we've had our difficulties but you're such a good girl that I know I know I must have done something somewhere right what did I do to deserve this treatment?

Cluck my feathers. Puff them up. Right so.

What's all this about? All this shit of you not doing this and that. The smell of it in here. Get up off your arse and do something with your life. Read a paper now and then. Or will you spend your whole life stacking shelves?

I like it you said. I just like it, it's fun to watch them doing kicks. I'm sorry. I'll do better. I will. I. Don't be angry with me.

Just get off your arse and pull your weight.

That night sitting sitting room. With The Irish Times. Flick through it.

What do you think of that? And see this picture? See yer one?

Flick again. Ho. Sniff.

And what is that?

Read the paper.

Since when do you? Who got you up to that?

She did.

Did she now and what gave her the right?

Now miss. What are you playing at? Come back here splashing orders saying who's doing what. Oh thinking you're so grand. Off up there at some college. Looking down your nose at me and your brother. We get on. Just fine without you here. Fine without you. And I'll thank you not to interfere. The cheek.

The cheek of it. I've had a-fucking-nough of this.

I went off back to there and my best friend.

Drink this. Go here. See him. Do that. No bits pieces left unsaid. And truth now tell the truth we say. Her father felt her up. It makes her red and cry. I tell her. Kinds of stuff. About you.

My brother's shy.

Patterns of the truth but not it. I. Hold on to that. If she wants to spew it out, that's for her. Not me too. No need to say. What is there to say?

I met a man. I met a man. I let him throw me round the bed. And smoked, me, spliffs and choked my neck until I said I was dead. I met a man who took me for walks. Long ones in the country. I offer up. I offer up in the hedge. I met a man I met with her. She and me and his friend to bars at night and drink champagne and bought me chips at every teatime. I met a man with condoms in his pockets. Don't use them. He loves children in his heart. No. I met a man who knew me once. Who said come back marry me live on my farm. No. I met a man who was a priest I didn't I did. Just as well as many another one would. I met a man. I met a man. Who said he'd pay me by the month. Who said he'd keep me up in style and I'd be waiting when he arrived. No is what I say. I met a man who hit me a smack. I met a man who cracked my arm. I met a man who said what are you doing out so late at night. I met a man. I met a man. And I lay down. And slapped and cried and wined and dined. I met a man and many more and I didn't know you at all.

So she called me.

Your grandfather's. Died. In his sleep.

Oh Mammy.

That old bastard.

Those fields. Filled up with rain. Even cows drown here.
Even sheep. Even people if they're lucky. If Jesus was here
he'd have gone. Running. Screaming with his sandals all
flapping in through the cow shit.

Inside people there I've not known before. That's a whole
ocean of cousins alone. Hordes.

Will you have a sandwich?

And uncles. Now with my mouth full of egg. I have not
thought. Oh God. Of. Right. Here.

Well my girl you're all grown up. That's changed a shade.
Out of a bottle no doubt. I can always tell. Say hello to
your uncle over there.

And I do.

Put out the silver candlesticks have we white candles?

No.

I'll go out and get.

I'll give her a lift I hear uncle say.

Bring back Jameson's while you're at it. No. Bushmills.
Something like that.

Put your belt on. Long time no see.

You've grown so much. You've grown up. You're a
woman now.

I have. I am. I suppose I am.

I have often thought about you and. What we did. What
I did. I did then.

So are you feeling guilty?

What? About what?

About that time when you fucked me?

Yes. About that. I feel guilty and I am.

Because I was thirteen?

I shouldn't have done it and I know that.

But you did.

I did.

Fuck me.

Fuck you.

And did you enjoy it?

Yes.

Why did you if you knew it was so wrong?

I couldn't somehow not. You were like. You were like. It doesn't matter. There is no good thing to say.

Well then. That's that.

And I suppose there's been others?

Yes.

You haven't damaged me if you're afraid of. Haven't soiled my goods.

You're angry.

I'm not. I am not. I.

You've got beautiful.

Well you know growing up does that.

Morning mass and the funeral. A good man and a sound man. He's buried. Under the muck. Go on there get into your hole. Amen. And. Amen.

Well now we must meet up again not wait till someone dies the next time. They all neigh and say the same but I go out.

I'm going he said. Jesus. I want. I want.

Want what?

I can't do without this. Without you. Again. I want. I. Want you again. Yes or no he says. Yes or no.

Will I? Can I? Do I want? I.

Do you have a pen?

PART IV
Extreme Unction

Jesus that. Stink of that. City when I got off the train.

God you look desperate. What have you been up to?

My grandfather died.

She and I. Going mad. Back to the books to the fucks I forget we are going round and around again.

No sign of him. Uncle. And just as well.

The phone rings.

What? What are you saying?

What's happened now what?

Where are you ringing from?

Swish swish all the hospital doors in the world sound the same.

Oh thank God you've come thank God thank God. He's just being examined. You and me we'll wait out here.

I expect prayers to come. But they don't. Just we'll lose him and I know we will.

We'll not Mammy. Mammy we won't.

Down we go.

Sitting prop in the bed. You. With some bowl of pudding with your wobble hand eat. You look like five again.

Now what have you done? Gone fell over like an eejit.
Cracked your head.

They come.

It's not so good as we had hoped.

We think it's spread too far into the brain. We can't
operate.

What nothing can be done?

We'll chemo it a little bit. Might shrink. I'm sorry.
Perhaps about a year.

And the blender go off inside me. Suck my heart my
lungs my brains in. She gulping softly at the air.

Did he say I could go home soon, now I'm alright?

Yes he. Why don't you have a little sleep? That's right.
Go on. Have a little snooze. You'll be fine. You'll be fine.

I called him then in the hospital foyer. Phone pissing
money coin p's away.

Is that you? Christ why are you calling me.

Pip by pip pip.

I. Please come and save me please pull me from.

2

I wanted you to come I say.

Uncle and I and. My fillet self.

My My My brother.

Stop. I'm here now. I'm here. Come for you.

He pull up my skirt. Put his hand between my legs.

43

Put yourself on me then, in me. Pull all other things out. Do whatever you want.

Take me stitch by stitch. Off. As though he knew and unwound it. I remember.

And I give him such a wide space to fill. Such a great white and empty room. I am.

In the evening when he can kiss me with all his tongue. I am evened. He says he's got an evening flight.

Say hello to my aunt for me.

3

I come down to see you again. Now every weekend.

You are saying doesn't it look like a when we were little day? High sky and snackish air.

It does.

We walk so slow for you.

Knock knock.

We came to lend our support. We heard about your brother. The ministry missionary fellowship. Praise the Lord praise the Lord above.

We're not Christians you know, that way. The way like you are I say. We're Catholics. Christians go and shite.

They're here all the time. Saying prayers you know and lay on hands. I don't like that much. I get. Scared. Of die of dying of go to hell.

You're not going anywhere. At all. Understand me. Listen. Don't believe that all. That nonsense rubbish crap it is.

They're eejits. And I say, you'll be fine. You'll be fine.

Oh God. That retch. Just retching retching on my hands my clothes skirt. The much of it stench coming back out more and more.

Sorry I'm sorry sorry.

It's fine it's fine. The chemo's working. There now. Lie now. Do you think you can lie down? You're fine. You're grand.

And where have you been?

Been with Christ. Your brother will be fine.

Christ Mammy.

Ah. You'd do well.

Now Mammy I've got to go out now. Need a little break. Just. He was so ill. Down the pub. Yes I gave. One two friends. A call.

I go down and out alright. I know my way. That road. Up that road and in. The quiet trees. The dark.

In the thicket. The bushes. The hedge.

Hello girleen.

Some man.

If I had a chance. To start again. I wouldn't. I'd do this. I would. But every day. Every day.

4

He looks at me. Uncle. Take me backwards into that dark room.

It's you I want and not all this shit.

Just hit me on the face.

No. I don't want this he says I don't want.

Just till my nose bleeds and that will be enough.

Jesus I feel sick.

But I am rush with feeling.

He thinks he's bad when he fucks me now. And so he is. I'm better though. In fact I'm almost best.

Jesus Christ oh Jesus Christ what happened your face? Did someone beat you up? Did he do that to you? Did he do that? You are fucked-up in the head. Do you hear me? So wrapped up in yourself in your brother and your uncle and fucking weird fucking.

Shut up. Shut up. Shut up.

Get that you says Mammy. Don't want to talk she says.

Hello. Who? I see. No my mother no. She doesn't want. No. You better talk to me. It's fine. I'm. Yes. Sitting down.

I under. I understand.

Knocking tat the door she is.

Shhh he's sleeping.

Mammy.

Let's sit down. Bow our our. Intercede. Implored thy
intercession was left unaided. Fly unto thee oh virgin of
virgins my mother. To thee do we come.

You listen to me. It's me. You. Listen to me. Mammy. For
once. One time.

But graciously hear and answer us.

Do you hear me? Me. You can't believe it away. Listen to
what I've. Got. To. Say. He's going to die.

Don't say that. Don't tell him. He'll give up. He'll lose
his. Faith and then we're really done.

Faith won't save him. He's a right to know.

I'm his mother I forbid.

He has a right to know he's going to die.

Then let it be on your head. Let it be on you. If you he
dies let it be on you.

Mammy.

Don't tell.

Mammy.

You heard what I said.

City. I walk the street. Who's him? That man. Who's him
there having a looking at me he. Look at my. Tits. Ssss.
Fuck that. No. Will. Not that. Not. That. But. If I want
to then I can do. And it would fill me up fine. And I. I do.
Do it. Take him back with me. Give him. The word. I
want that. Hurt me. Until I am outside pain.

That's the end of the end of that and I won't be seeing
doing. Fucking. No more. No fucking much. Shut your
legs. I won't be. I won't.

47

I say to him Uncle. That's it. Don't come, I think, any more.

Just come to my hotel once?

No.

I'll do. My. For you. My best for you.

PART V
The Stolen Child

I'm in. The house. I am here. Minding.

Above I hear her turning. Hit her headboard with her prayers. Why don't you shut up? No now. You're here to care. You're clean here. You're calm and kind.

Wipe the kitchen over. This J-cloth. This scouring pad.

She comes. All tidy down.

Oh. I see what you're at madam. Never bothered here and now. Don't forget I'm the mother here.

I. Didn't.

I called your aunt. Your uncle and aunt. Asked them to come.

What?

Just keep yourself to yourself while they're here. Nobody wants to hear your cheek.

You and me sit. Watching TV.

What'll I make you?

Beans on toast.

I look at you. Good to see the smile of you.

Beans on toast. I'll. Just sit there I'll bring them in.

I don't know what to say says our aunt.

I'm so glad you're here. I'm just worn out.

There there.

Come on in and sit down you must be exhausted from the flight. Show your uncle their room you.

What did you come for?

I want you.

Not here all that's done.

I want.

No.

You to leave with me.

Fuck you.

Around that dinner table. Stuffing all our mouths shut. She aunt going nack nack nack. Those eyes uncle eyes eat all things off my skin. He looks through the table smile at me.

I'm going out.

Where you?

See you I.

Out of here.

I go into the black of trees. Moss wet ground. I want the. Earth. My legs spread wide.

Come the fucking soldiers for me. Stink I want.

Hello you there they say. You know it's not safe to be hanging around here in the dark.

I know you I say. From before.

Hmm. Oh yes. Nice young girleen. Say how you'd like come in the dark dirt with me?

Ah fine fuck fine. There we go now hey. Ah. There's it. Ow I say. Ah ha ha ha.

Sounds. Someone's come.

Yee haa girleen. Come on. Come on girleen.

There Uncle. Turn.

What you doing? To that girl? You fucking. Pervert. Fucking. Scum you.

What's it to you? says my fucker. Get off me she wanted it.

Kick him stomach.

Stop it I.

Fuck you.

He hit and hit him.

You bastard stinking fucking.

Stop Jesus stop it I wanted him to.

And that man on the ground. Pass out.

Spit on him.

You fucking pervert you fucking dare. She's my. And you, can't you keep your knickers to yourself. My love. He says. My love for. Love for you.

Is nothing.

We get to the house. He threw me in the door.

Stop playing up. Your brother is ill. You selfish madam. She's up to all sorts, that one.

And they clapped they loved they worshipped him. I picked up sticks out of my hair. Dirt up off my tongue.

I went in. You sleep. You sleeping.

I think your face the very best. When we were we were we were young. When you were little and I was girl. Once upon a time. I'll mind you mind you.

I won't. I swear. Leave you alone.

I'm doctor from the hospice. Tell me how you feeling?

You say. I'm so tired now. All the time I. Wish I'd watch television I'd play some games with the other boys if ever they came round.

I.

Shush there, let him tell me. How do you think you are yourself?

I. Haven't I?

Haven't you what?

Cancer somehow in there.

You do, I'm very sorry to say.

Will I give it to my children when I grow up?

You won't.

That's good.   When am I going to get well?

You're not. I'm sorry to.

Am I   Am I going to die?

You are.

Sooner or later doctor?

Sooner. I'm sorry. I'm so sorry to have to say.

I'm going to die then. Now. I'm going to die.

Yes. Is there anything you want anyone to do?

No.

Is there anything that you'd like to?

Say sorry.

What?

I am sorry to my mother and I'm sorry to my sister. I'm sorry to you for this dying and all the things I've done.

Oh no oh no oh don't do that or say those things that are no matter any more.

Don't be sorry to me.

I want to.

Don't. Shush silent night.

Fill my mouth up with bedspread. Fill the air out. Stop the. The coming in. And your hand on it. Down on my hair. You're crying and I am.

There there

You are saying to me.

There there there.

Death falling through the room, sucking all words from air for us.

And you said

Why you crying? Why's everyone crying here? I was asleep and now everyone's crying.

She mother says there's no reason in the wide wide world.

At the door. Her whisper saying tell me when?

Maybe weeks. One or two. Not any more.

My son my son. My child my baby my boy my boy. She puts her arms around me. Oh my little. My boy my boy.

My mother. Feel the. Strange and I am comfort there. I am the. Right. I am the right thing.

These hours days. And everybody. All around here. Tapping all the time out.

Hello morning my love.

And kiss your face. That's warm. And hard with sleep to the touch. Closed. Open your eyes. Your mouth rattles. I know this. I know what it means.

Doorbell rings. Come the holy holy things. No no not today not not them.

They troop. Them large them heap of things and come in smile and go cluster in your room.

There bring more chairs down.

Don't move. I stand.

Get them.

I won't.

Or you can stay in your room.

And leave my brother? I won't do that.

Go and get or get out and get to hell.

I bring one five six seven in.

Eat my butter bread across the table from him uncle.

Look at me he say. Sorry. For this. For your mother doing. For. Today.

Kiss the side of my face.

Give me your dishes. Go on in to your brother. I'll do them up for you.

Their hands laid upon. Bless everywhere on you.

Excuse me. Move out of my way I'm. My brother.

I hold your hand.

Keep off my breath my head and your rising falling shoulder whisper to you I'm here as well as fecking eejits. Don't forget that I am here.

Today. Is still here. I'll be. At your. Right. Hand. You are my.

Bite.

And all your. Sudden body. Where's the. It. Comes for you. Please don't go no. Not. Go. I. Please don't leave. There's the. Air flying out. Your eyes on me. They. You are.

Silent.

Breath.

Lungs go out. See the world out.

You finish that breath. Song breath.

You are gone out tide. And you close. Drift. Silent eyes. Goodbye.

My. lllllllllllllllll. Love my. Brother no.

He's gone. My.

Done. And. Quiet.

And.

Gone.

Who am I talking to? Who am I talking to now?

I run. Run the run the.

I'm here. In the dark. Where I come to see the. What's.
It's the devil. I do here.

Hear the. Shush. Angel save me. He comes and comes till
I see. Through the broken trees.

I've been waiting for you.

That man who say girleen girleen like a song.

Thanks for all my pain. Slap.

My brother.

Shut up. Shut up.

My brother died. He's died he's.

I don't care a single fuck about. Where's your uncle is he
here? Is he here?

Thrash. Screaming.

Shut up.

Fling rubbish thrown I am am I I. Falt. Where until I
crack. Break my. Face. Head. Where on the back of my
head on the back of my back my back crack that's my
eyes fucking up with tears.

Stop stop it you are I don't want.

Spread fucking open up you sick fucking stupid bitch
want the fuck you just like this.

No. Get off.

They're off fuck knickers off. Thighs in claws I vice. Rip
m open. Don't break me open face open. Crushing I hear
boines on done he up me fuck me. Done fuk me open he
dine done on me. Done done Til he hye happy fucky
shoves upo comes ui. Kom shitting ut h mith fking kmg

I'm fking cmin up you.

Retch I. Retch I. Dinnerandtea I choke mny. Up my.
Thrtoat I. Slash the fuck the rank the sick up me sick up
he and sticks his fingers in my mouth. Piull my mth he
pull m mouth with him fingers pull the side of my mouth
til I no. Tear my mouth.

There bitch there bithc there there

Stranlge me strangle

How you like it how you think it is fun

Grouged breth sacld my lungs til I. Puk blodd over me
frum. mY nose my mOuth I. VOMit. Clear. CleaR. He
stopS up gETs. Stands uP. Look. And I breath. And I
breath my. I make.

You like those feelings do you now. Thanks to your uncle
for that like the best fuck I ever had.

HoCk SPIT me. Kicks. uPshes me over

Thanks for fuck you thanks for that I.   hear his
walking crunching. Foot foot. Go.   Him Away.

And I am. Done with this done. My work is. I've done
my I should do. I've done the this time really well. And
best of. It was the best of. I fall I felled. I banged my face
head I think. Time for somewhere. Isgoinghome.

I get there I get. Go in.

Not you I. Forget. You are. Gone.

Oh Lord God. What happened you? What happened your face?

They come like locust clusters of bees on me land on me.

And she my mother look at that what. Eyes burst with rage she.

What have you done?

I fell I hit my head I fell I got my mouth I caught my pulled it on a bramble pulled it on.

What are you on about? Your lies and lies are. You're a state. Go she says and have a bath. Get out of my sight.

I climb the up the. Hurt. Stairs. I go. Behind I hear them close your door and pray.

Do not be afraid – I will save you.

I have called you by name – you are mine.

When you pass through deep water, I will be with you; your troubles will not overwhelm you.

For I am the Lord your God.

I turn the bath light on I see I think that fuck punge of my face. Door handle turn. Don't come in it's. For him the who's there uncle looking in at you. No. At me.

Jesus Christ you're green. What have you done?

He stretch his hand out. Touch my hair. The. Dirt in it. Picks.

You done, you done this to yourself this? This?

Stroke my. Don't do that I.

Shush love shush you now.

I'll mind you.

No.

Shush there.

Lift my skirt up I think knicker hands. Runs hands on score thighs dirt.

I'll take care of you.

No don't.

Shhhh. Don't let everybody hear. I lo I lo. I'll take care of you. Let me.

Oh no no no no no. I don't want. Want.

Quiet pet.

There he does it. Stick it ionthe don'tinside

sthroughmythrough

Can't smell this room.

Kiss my girl my poor poor girl. Take care of you. I'll mind you now and tuck his thing. Love now I'm going down. See if I can help your mother. Keep everything normal isn't that right? You should go to bed. It's a long and terrible day for you.

He. Sit me on the bath. I hold on there.

Now love.

Tight until he's gone.

Stag i can't stan i cn.an't stan i fall down on the splish of the water run it. See my invisible face.

What he takes. What he takes is the what there is of me.

Wake. My everything sting and swollen.

I go into your room. You are breathing no not. Like stone. I kiss the all. Wrong head poor head. Was yours. Hold.

In the kitchen no move no one. Everyone quiet is sip their tea.

Is your face sore?

Not too.

Teach you what. Teach you go walking all times of day and night.

Yes Mammy.

You're a disgrace. If your father was. Sit up while I'm talking. Sit up I said. Your brother's dead my girl. Your brother's dead and all you can think about is. Before everyone. Before everyone you came here and displayed yourself looking for sympathy. From me? From me? You dirty.

Don't now our uncle says.

You keep your nose out if nothing else. I can't even look at you. I haven't wanted you in my home. But I allowed you because I thought you were making amends. But not you. Of course not. Selfish to the last. You couldn't even let your brother's wake pass without making a show of yourself, showing everyone your contempt. Well my girl, you may look down your nose at my beliefs and friends but I wasn't out throwing myself on every man passing while my brother was dying. You are disgusting. You are.

Sick in the head. How you've lived. This filth you've made of yourself. So now your good kind brother is gone and God forgive me but it's true. I almost wish it was you lying there in that box. You. And not. My. Son.

Where you going?

For a walk. Down.

You be back here in an hour and you be washed and dressed and clean there're people coming. And cover that bruise, it's the very least you can do. You're a disgrace.

I am gone gone gone.

There's water I see. Come to know. Touched and loved and ripped here.

I step in water on my cold feet.

Strip pain all the parts off me. Wash away. Wash into the deep with it.

The black I swim. The coldest water. Deepest mirror of the past and in it I am. Fine look because I see you under. Because we are very young. And we are very clean here like when we wash our hands. When we're in the rain.

And I know what you say. Come on you say. Come with. Come down. You tell. You tell me your name and tell me the truth this time.

And you say. Say it once. Hail holy queen. Poor banished children of Eve and you say oh sacred heart of Jesus I place all my trust in thee. There is no other one. No person more inside for fuck for work for. For I'm twenty now when you were gone.

Rise up the lake above me. I'll take your hand. Brother me. Clean here. I'm. Tired. Let it.

Go there.

Struggle down.

We are down down down.

And under water lungs grow. Flowing in. That choke of.
Eyes and nose and throat. Where uncle did. No. Gone
away. Where mother speak. Is deaf my ears. Hold tight
to me. Will I say? For you to hear? Alone. My name is.
Water. All alone. My name. The plunge is faster. The
deeper cold is coming in. What's left? What's left behind?
It is. My name for me. My I.

Turn. Look up. Bubble from my mouth drift high. Blue
tinge lips. Floating hair. Air famished eyes. Brown water
turning into light. There now. There now. That just was
life. And now.

What?

My name is gone.